Tudor Travellers

Haydn Middleton

Ginn

Into the Unknown

Five hundred years ago, life was very different. People in Europe knew very little about the rest of the world. Some even believed the earth was **flat!** Then brave sea captains took to the high seas, crossing vast oceans in tiny, wooden ships. They found new lands, new people and odd new things to eat.

As you travel through these pages, write down and keep your answers to each QUIZ question. (Remember, the answers are in the book!) Let's set sail!

The Tudor family ruled England from 1485 to 1603. We call this period 'Tudor times', so the people who went exploring were ... **Tudor Travellers!**

Henry VII
1485–1509

Henry VIII
1509–1547

Edward VI
1547–1553

Mary I
1553–1558

Elizabeth I
1558–1603

3

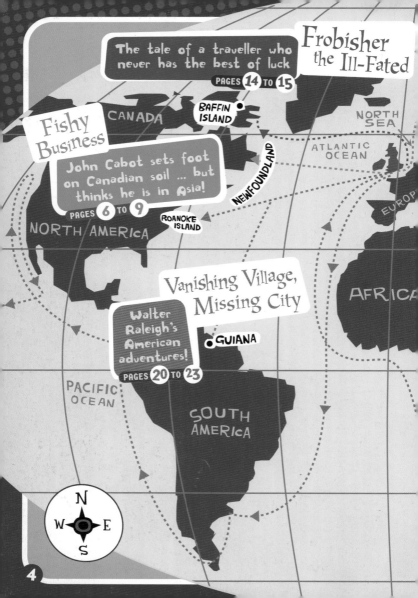

Frobisher the Ill-Fated

The tale of a traveller who never has the best of luck

Fishy Business

John Cabot sets foot on Canadian soil ... but thinks he is in Asia!

Vanishing Village, Missing City

Walter Raleigh's American adventures!

CANADA

BAFFIN ISLAND

NORTH SEA

ATLANTIC OCEAN

NEWFOUNDLAND

EUROPE

NORTH AMERICA

ROANOKE ISLAND

AFRICA

GUIANA

PACIFIC OCEAN

SOUTH AMERICA

N W E S

RUSSIA

● MOSCOW

Lost in the North

Richard Chancellor travels first by ship and then by sledge.

PAGES **10** TO **13**

ASIA

INDIA

PACIFIC OCEAN

Beware the Dragon

Francis Drake just keeps on sailing!

PAGES **16** TO **19**

INDIAN OCEAN

Follow the arrows to find out where the Tudor Travellers went! Anchors away!

Fishy Business

What lies beyond the coasts of Britain? Before Tudor times, no one was sure. Some English fishermen believed there were islands with big cities on them. But better still, they told stories of enormous fish swimming around the islands! A sea captain called John Cabot heard these fishy stories. In 1497, he set sail with 18 English sailors, to see if they were true.

Name John Cabot

Nationality Italian, working for England's King Henry VII

Lived From around 1455 to 1498

Fun Fact King Henry was so pleased with Cabot's findings, he gave him £20. This was more than most Tudor men earned in a year!

Did fish this big really exist beyond Britain? Or were they just fishermen's dreams?

After 35 days at sea, Cabot's ship came to a coast. Cabot went ashore and declared the 'new found land' now belonged to England. His men caught huge amounts of fish, but they were no bigger than back home! Enormous fish were just fishermen's dreams after all. *But where, exactly, was Cabot?*

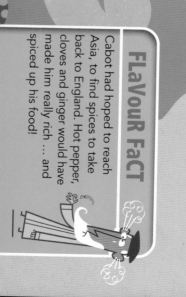

FLaVouR FaCT

Cabot had hoped to reach Asia, to find spices to take back to England. Hot pepper, cloves and ginger would have made him really rich ... and spiced up his food!

To the new found land

The **Matthew**, John Cabot's ship, was only 24 metres long and just 6 metres wide.

Cabot thought that he had landed in an empty part of Asia. In fact, he was the first sea captain from Europe to reach the land we now call Canada. And the part he reached is now called … Newfoundland.

Lost in the North

Tudor Travellers sailed to India to buy spices such as pepper and ginger. They had to sail right around Africa to get there – a major mission! So, in 1553, Richard Chancellor went exploring with two ships, hoping to find a quicker route to India.

Name Richard Chancellor

Nationality English

Lived From around 1515 to 1556

RUSSIAN EMPIRE **1555**

Fun Fact Chancellor made his sailors wear funky sky-blue coloured uniforms!

The ruler of Russia was Emperor Ivan IV, nicknamed Ivan the Terrible. Ivan had a serious temper problem. He killed his own son just for annoying him.

Chancellor set off across the icy North Sea, but soon his two ships lost contact. Chancellor sailed on alone and came to a strange, cold land. Local people helped him travel inland, often on sledges, for 1500 miles. At last, he came to a wonderful city where the country's ruler lived. The city was called Moscow and the country was … Russia.

Emperor Ivan was keen for Russia and England to become friendly, so he welcomed Chancellor. He knew the English made very powerful cannons and he wanted some for himself! Ivan was also keen to find himself an Empress, so he asked England's queen, Elizabeth I, to marry him. She politely said NO!

FRoZeN FaCT

What happened to Chancellor's second ship? Its crew got lost during the bitter northern winter. This included five long weeks when the sun never rose. The next summer, all 70 bodies were found ... frozen.

QUIZ If Elizabeth I had agreed to marry Ivan the Terribl

Richard Chancellor never reached India by
sailing north. But he did make lots of friends
on his journey and soon started selling all sorts
of goods to Russia. He sold them woollen
clothes and, of course, **awesome cannons**. The
Russians sold him … ropes! Why ropes? They
came in handy for English shipbuilders, who
fitted them to new ocean-going ships.

Frobisher the Ill-Fated

1 At age 14, Martin Frobisher was already helping out on dangerous trading voyages to Africa.

2 He then led three expeditions to find a westward route to Asia over the top of America. Each time, Frobisher failed to find a way through.

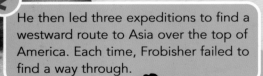

3 Frobisher brought back some people from North America called Inuits. These were the first Inuits to visit England. Sadly, they could not cope with England's climate and soon died.

4 Frobisher finally became a hero in 1588 for helping to beat off a Spanish sea-attack on England. But in 1596, he was killed in a sea-attack on France.

Beware the Dragon

In 1577, sea captain Francis Drake sailed out from Plymouth and did not return for three years! He was the first person to sail around the world and he came back with news about lands overseas … oh, and a huge fortune!

Name Francis Drake

Nationality English

Lived From around 1543 to 1596

WORLD TOUR 1577 to 1580

Fun Fact Drake had musicians on board his ship, to play to him at mealtimes!

Drake's ship, the **Golden Hind**, was just 23 metres long – with over 70 men crammed on board!

Hope I don't need the toilet in the night!

Drake and his officers had small rooms to themselves on board the ship. The rest of the crew squeezed together below deck to sleep. There was very little headroom, but Tudor men were shorter than today. Their average height was only about 1.63 metres!

During his world trip, Drake and his crew attacked a Spanish ship carrying American gold and silver. They seized treasure worth £140,000; a massive amount of money in 1579. Queen Elizabeth I of England was extremely pleased with Drake and made him Sir Francis Drake. She also let him keep £10,000, with £10,000 more for his crew.

Francis ✳✳✳✳✳ had his own room on the ship.

Drake and his crew on the attack! They would seize treasure, but usually let the attacked ship sail away.

FiRe-BReaTHiNG FaCT

Drake's Spanish enemies called him El Draque – the Dragon. They thought he used a 'magic mirror' to tell him where to find their ships.

while his crew slept below ✳✳✳✳.

Vanishing Village, Missing City

There were 90 men, 17 women and 9 children on board the ship sailing to Roanoke Island.

In 1587, John White set sail with a ship full of Tudor men, women and children, bound for Roanoke Island on the North American coast. This was no normal expedition. Roanoke was to be their new home. Like the Native Americans who lived on Roanoke already, the newcomers built a village, planted crops and fished in the sea.

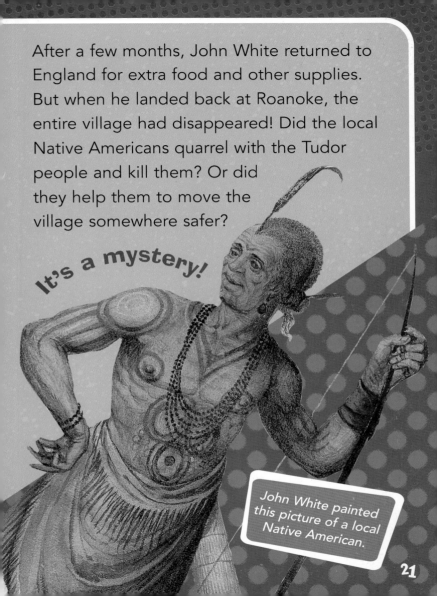

After a few months, John White returned to England for extra food and other supplies. But when he landed back at Roanoke, the entire village had disappeared! Did the local Native Americans quarrel with the Tudor people and kill them? Or did they help them to move the village somewhere safer?

It's a mystery!

John White painted this picture of a local Native American.

GUIANA ★ 1595

Name Walter Raleigh

Nationality English

Lived From around 1552 to 1618

Fun Fact Raleigh may have introduced an exotic American snack to Tudor England. The potato!

The man who had planned the expedition to Roanoke was called Walter Raleigh. In 1595, he led a new expedition to search for Eldorado. This was a city made of pure gold somewhere in South America – or so Raleigh had heard. For two months, he battled through jungle up the Orinoco River, where at last he found … nothing at all!